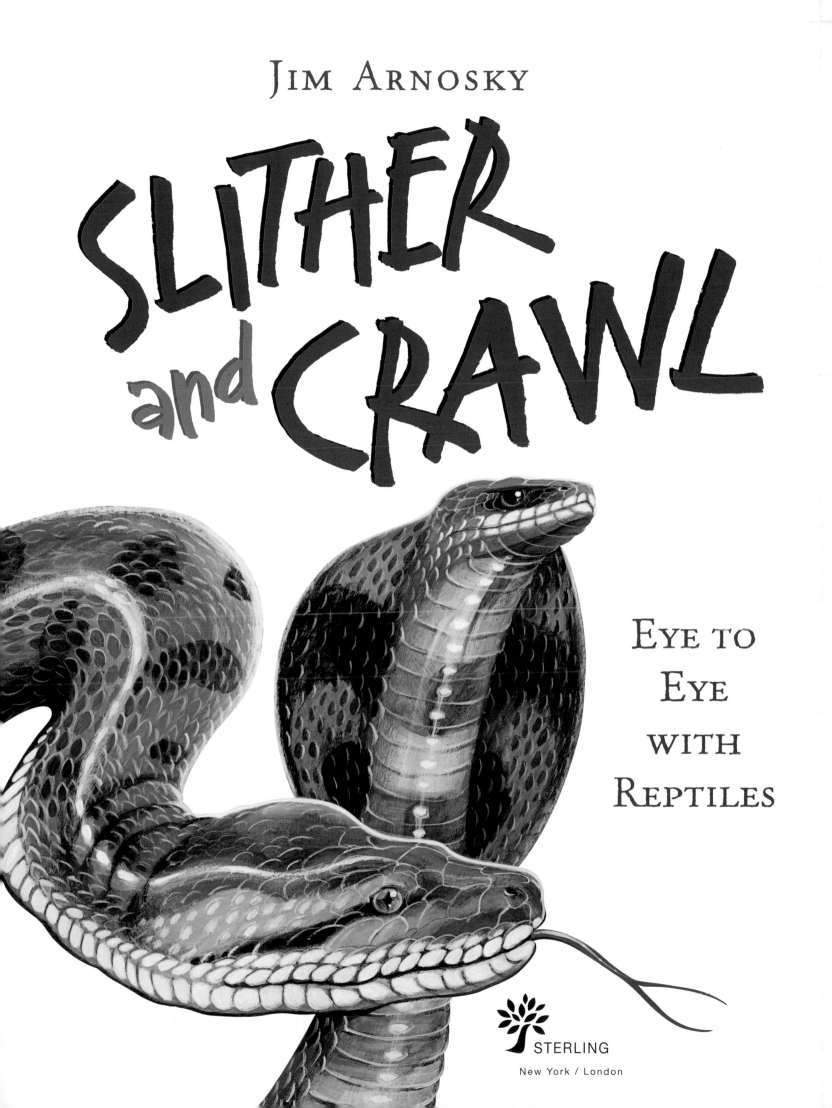

Jim Arnosky

SLITHER and CRAWL

Eye to Eye with Reptiles

STERLING

New York / London

For Brendan, Connor, & Liam

STERLING and the distinctive Sterling logo
are registered trademarks of Sterling Publishing Co., Inc.

Library of Congress Cataloging-in-Publication Data
Arnosky, Jim.
  Slither and crawl / Jim Arnosky.
    p. cm.
  Includes bibliographical references.
  ISBN 978-1-4027-3986-6
  1. Reptiles--Juvenile literature. I. Title.
  QL644.2.A76 2009
  597.9--dc22

                                2008022493

10 9 8 7 6 5 4 3 2 1

Published by Sterling Publishing Co., Inc.
387 Park Avenue South, New York, NY 10016
Text and illustrations © 2009 by Jim Arnosky
Distributed in Canada by Sterling Publishing
c/o Canadian Manda Group, 165 Dufferin Street
Toronto, Ontario, Canada M6K 3H6
Distributed in the United Kingdom by GMC Distribution Services
Castle Place, 166 High Street, Lewes, East Sussex, England BN7 1XU
Distributed in Australia by Capricorn Link (Australia) Pty. Ltd.
P.O. Box 704, Windsor, NSW 2756, Australia

The artwork for this book was prepared using pencil and acrylic paints.
Display lettering created by Kirsten Horel
Designed by Lauren Rille

Sterling ISBN 978-1-4027-3986-6

For information about custom editions, special sales, premium and corporate purchases,
please contact Sterling Special Sales Department at 800-805-5489 or specialsales@sterlingpublishing.com.

Contents

ALLIGATOR

Introduction

Growing up in Pennsylvania, I dreamed of wild places where snakes slithered across jungle trails, lizards climbed on twisted branches of trees, and alligators crawled out of the water onto lush green banks. Reptiles have always captured my imagination in a way no other animals do.

Reptiles are cold-blooded. They cannot warm themselves internally the way birds and mammals can. Reptiles find sun to warm up and shade to cool down.

Reptiles include turtles, snakes, lizards, and crocodilians. In the United States, there are many different species of turtles, snakes, and lizards, but only two native crocodilians: crocodiles and alligators. Most of the reptiles in this book are native to North America. A few are native to other parts of the world. I have included them to give you an idea of just how broad a variety of reptiles there are.

Many reptiles are harmless. Just as many are dangerous. Some are venomous (poisonous). When I'm watching dangerous reptiles in the wild, I use binoculars or a telephoto camera lens so that I can see them clearly, but from a safe distance. You can get a close-up view of all the reptiles in this book just by looking at my life-size paintings. So belly down on the ground, eye to reptilian eye, and read all about these fascinating animals that slither and crawl.

Jim Arnosky

Loggerhead sea turtle

Chuckwalla lizard

Yellow Rat Snake

5

BANDED WATER SNAKE

BROWN ANOLE

LIFE-SIZE SNAKES

DIAMONDBACK RATTLESNAKE
Rattlesnakes, copperheads, and cottonmouths are pit vipers. The heat-sensing pits between the eyes and nostrils of the snakes aid in locating prey.

Venom is primarily used for subduing prey. Before using its venom to defend itself, a snake may try to scare off threats by coiling tightly, hissing loudly, or even striking out but not biting. Cobras spread their skin hoods to appear larger. Rattlesnakes shake their rattles as a warning.

COPPERHEAD

COTTONMOUTH
MOCCASIN

KINGSNAKE
The only snake that regularly kills and eats rattlesnakes

CORAL SNAKE

BLUE RACER
Nonvenomous but aggressive and will bite you

ORANGE RAT SNAKE
There are also black rat snakes and yellow rat snakes.

GARTER SNAKE

TREE BOA (SOUTH AMERICA)

Boas are constrictors. They squeeze the life out of prey animals before swallowing them.

NORTHERN WATER SNAKE

Water snakes will bite without warning.

COBRA (ASIA AND AFRICA)

When confronted, cobra will lift the fro[nt] third of its body off the ground and strike from that position.

ANACONDA (SOUTH AMERI[CA])

The anaconda, the largest snake [in] the world, can grow to 35 feet [in] length and weigh over 250 pou[nds]

Rattlesnake warning
"Go away!"

Snakes

I was crawling on my elbows toward an amber-colored trout pool. Suddenly, right in front of me, a banded water snake looped down from the lowest branch of a streamside tree. For a moment we were eye to eye. Then the snake dropped to the ground and slithered into the water.

Snakes are reptiles that have no limbs (legs). Snakes have scaly skin and jaws that unhinge to open wide and swallow prey whole. Snakes have no eyelids, but transparent skin protects the snake's eyes. Broad grasping belly scales enable snakes to crawl and climb. Belly, back, and head scales waterproof the snake's body and prevent it from losing the moisture it needs. The scales on a snake's back are either smooth or keeled, depending on the species. Keeled scales have a ridge down the center, like the keel on the bottom of a boat.

There are more than 2,500 species of snakes in the world. While most begin life in the egg, many species are born live from the mother. As a snake grows, it periodically sheds its skin. The old skin, dry and dull in color, loosens and peels off in one piece, giving way to more supple, brilliantly colored new skin.

A wide triangular head usually means a snake is venomous. The triangular shape allows space for a venom sac above each jaw. Venom from such sacs is injected into prey through hollow fangs when the snake bites. Not all species of venomous snakes have triangular heads. Coral snakes and cobras, for example, are venomous but have oval heads.

Rattlesnake skull showing hollow fangs. Fangs hinge back against roof of mouth when not biting.

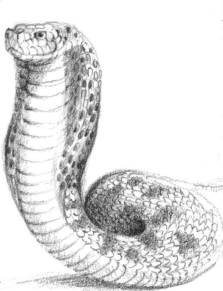

Hognose snake spreading neck skin to feign ferocity

Belly scales

Triangular head

Oval head

9

Iguana

Lizards

There are more species of lizards than of any other reptile, and they range in size from tiny to enormous. Snakes and lizards are classified together as scaled reptiles. Unlike snakes, most lizards have legs and eyelids. The limbless lizards known as glass lizards can be distinguished from snakes by the presence of eyelids. So if you think you are watching a snake, and it winks at you—think again.

Lizards live in deserts, wetlands, forests, fields, and even inside houses. Most eat insects. Some are vegetarians. A number of species are carnivorous. In general, lizards are harmless to humans. But any animal will bite when grabbed. The only venomous lizard in the United States is the Gila (pronounced HEE'-la) monster of the southwestern desert.

Lizard-watching is always hard-earned. It is not easy to get close to them. So many animals eat lizards that they simply cannot tolerate any approach. Lizards are all about getting away. They can run, climb, leap, and swim. Certain species have the added escape advantage of a disposable tail, leaving their pursuer with the detached tail while the lizard gets away to grow another.

Gecko

Skink

Typical Monitor Lizard

Leaping lizards!

Growing a new tail.

Gila Monster

KOMODO DRAGON
(INDONESIA)

GIGANTIC LIZARDS

Some lizard species grow to gigantic sizes. Green iguanas and Rhinoceros iguanas can grow to be 5 feet long or more. The largest lizards in the world are the monitor lizards, and the largest monitor lizard is the Komodo dragon of Indonesia. These giants grow to be 10 feet long, stand 2 feet tall at the shoulder, and weigh over 200 pounds.

RHINOCEROS IGUANA
(DOMINICAN REPUBLIC)
Rhinoceros iguanas are named for the hornlike bump on their foreheads.

GARTER SNAKES

Where Do Reptiles Go in Winter?

Though snakes, alligators, and crocodiles occasionally migrate to find water or better hunting areas, they, and many other reptiles, are not made for any long-distance seasonal migration. Unlike birds that can leave cold weather and fly hundreds, even thousands of miles to warmer places, reptiles have to stay put and endure the cold.

All reptiles react to cold weather by becoming sluggish and inactive. They find a place out of the wind and lie low. Crocodiles and alligators submerge most of their body in warm water or wallow in mud. Lizards retreat to available holes or crevices or simply cling to the innermost branches of trees. Turtles that live in water find warmer water. Land turtles dig in, retreat inside their shells, and tough out cold spells.

In places where winter is cold for months at a time, reptiles hibernate in mud or leaf litter. Some species hibernate communally, in rocky crevices or dens. Every winter garter snakes congregate to hibernate in a den under our house's stone foundation. It doesn't really feel like spring around our place until the snakes emerge, often all at once!

Alligator in muddy water.

GIANT TORTOISE

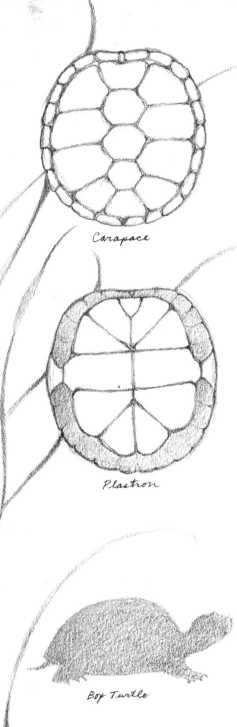

Carapace

Plastron

Box Turtle

Gopher Tortoise

Snapping Turtle

Turtles

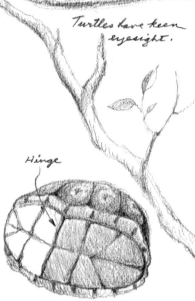

Snapping Turtle

Turtles have keen eyesight.

Tough and durable, turtles have been around since the dawn of the dinosaurs. There are 250 species of turtles living today.

Turtles are reptiles with protective shells made of strong bone—a top shell (carapace) and a bottom shell (plastron). Some turtles can hide completely inside their shells. The box turtle's hinged plastron clamps closed like a vacuum-sealed lid when the turtle pulls inside. Turtles that can only partially hide inside their shells have large front legs that block and protect their partially exposed heads.

There are land turtles and water turtles. Many species of land turtles have extra-tough skin and thick scales on their legs to protect them from bruises they might get when clambering over rugged terrain.

Tortoises are the largest land turtles. In dry country, they dig burrows in the sand. Besides providing protection from cuts and scratches while digging, a tortoise's thick skin helps to keep the tortoise from drying out.

Land turtles eat vegetation and insects. Swift and agile water turtles catch and eat fish. Big snapping turtles eat fish, swimming birds, and rodents.

Hinge

Box turtle's hinged bottom shell clamped closed. Turtle inside.

Sea Turtle

Some turtles can be identified by shape alone.

Softshell Turtle

DESERT TORTOISE
Desert tortoises often share their burrows with rattlesnakes.

BOX TURTLE

GIANT TORTOISE (GALAPAGOS ISLANDS)
This is the largest tortoise in the world—it can grow to be over 4 feet long and weigh more than 500 pounds.

ALLIGATOR SNAPPER
The alligator snapper has a pink, worm-like appendage on its tongue, which is used to lure fish to the turtle's powerful jaws.

SNAPPING TURTLE

LIFE-SIZE TURTLES

Reptiles are incredibly varied in size, color, and markings. Just look at the spectrum of colors and patterns in this small sampling of turtle species!

SPOTTED TURTLE

PAINTED TURTLE

MAP
TURTLE

DIAMONDBACK
TERRAPIN

SLIDER

SOFTSHELL TURTLE
The shells of softshell turtles are soft and flexible, but as tough as leather.

LOGGERHEAD SEA TURTLE AND PORK FISH

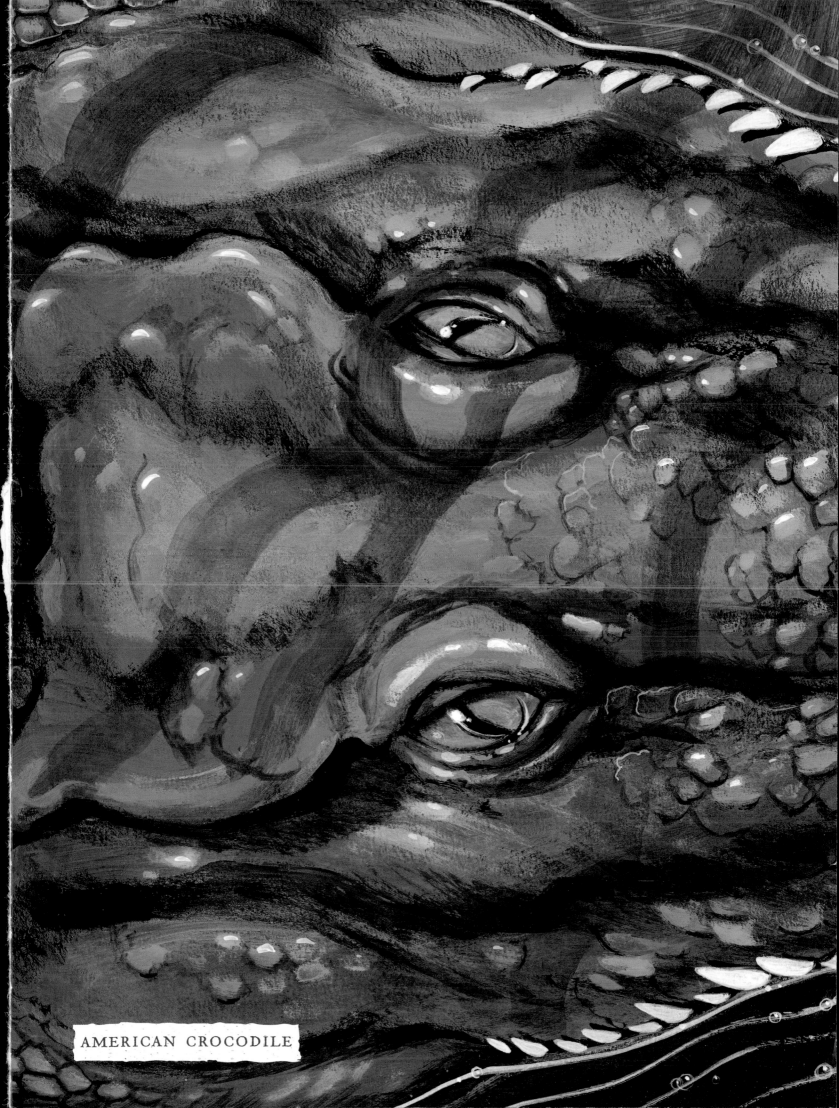

AMERICAN CROCODILE

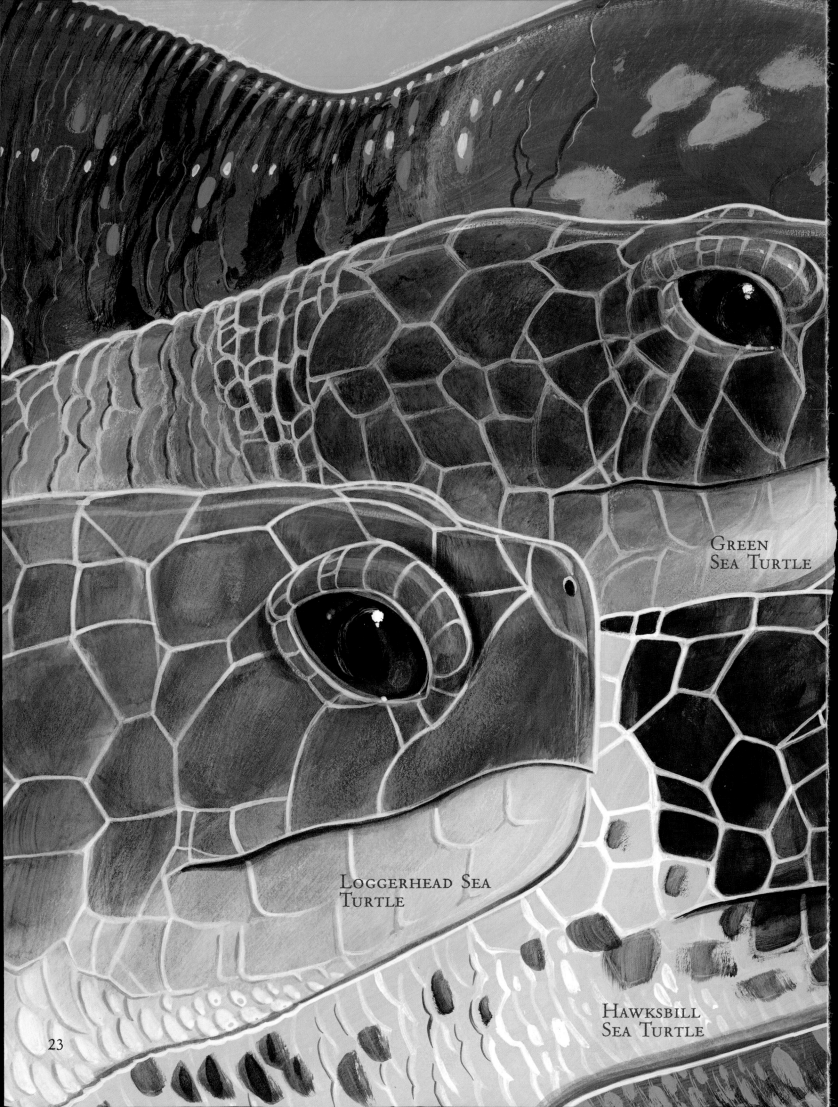

GREEN
SEA TURTLE

LOGGERHEAD SEA
TURTLE

HAWKSBILL
SEA TURTLE

LIFE-SIZE SEA TURTLES

LEATHERBACK
SEA TURTLE

All sea turtles are threatened by overhunting and accidental entrapment in commercial fishing nets. In the United States, many ancestral sea turtle nesting beaches are being watched in order to protect the turtle eggs and ensure that as many hatchlings as possible survive.

Sea Turtles

In the warm and shallow waters of Florida Bay, I often see sea turtles—mostly loggerheads—splashing after floating jellyfish. The turtles seem to be curious about the world around them. Once in a while, one will surface near my boat and look me over before diving back under.

Sea turtles are completely aquatic. They do not crawl out of the water to sun themselves the way freshwater turtles do.

Female sea turtles come on land only to lay and bury their eggs. They crawl onshore, dragging their heavy bodies on the sand. It is an arduous task. The weightlessness they feel in water is suddenly gone. Once they deposit their eggs, they abandon them and return to the sea. In all species of turtles, hatchlings fend for themselves. After baby sea turtles have dug themselves out of the nest, they rush to the relative safety of the sea. The males never again return to land.

As light and agile in the water as they are heavy and cumbersome on land, sea turtles feed on fish, crabs, mollusks, seaweed, algae, sponges, and jellyfish.

All sea turtles, except for the leatherback, have plated shells similar to the shells of land and freshwater turtles. The leatherback's leathery carapace is ridged, not plated.

Loggerhead, Ridley, Green, and Hawksbill Sea turtles all have plated shells.

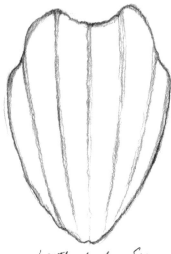

Leatherback Sea Turtles have ridged shells.

Leatherbacks grow to be eight feet long overall, and weigh 1000 to 1200 pounds.

Female Sea turtles crawl ashore to lay and bury their eggs.

Baby Sea turtles in the sea.

The leatherback's main diet consists of jellyfish!

25

Crocodiles and Alligators

Crocodile

Alligator

Crocodiles and alligators are the largest reptiles in the world. For 240 million years, crocodilians have reigned supreme in their watery environments. Throughout the southern United States, there are alligators living in freshwater and brackish water (a mixture of fresh and salt water). And in the saltwater bays and swamps along Florida's south coast, there are crocodiles. Both crocodiles and alligators can grow to be well over 13 feet in length.

Crocodiles and alligators are similar in many ways but different in some. Alligators are black and have broad snouts. Crocodiles are brown and have tapered snouts.

Dragonfly

Young crocodiles and alligators eat minnows and aquatic insects such as dragonflies. Adult crocs and gators eat anything they can catch, including people. I always keep a distance of at least 25 feet away from them on land. As slow as they may appear to be, crocodiles and alligators can run, lunge, and strike with alarming speed.

Both of these spectacular American reptiles became endangered species due to uncontrolled hunting. Once protected, they rebounded. Today in the United States, crocodiles and alligators are no longer endangered.

Baby Alligator
(actual size)
Yes, they actually do appear
to be smiling!

Alligator and Crocodile babies
enjoy the security of a fiercely
protective mother always
somewhere close.

LIFE-SIZE
AMERICAN CROCODILE
AND YOUNG

The crocodile pictured here is more than 11 feet in length
and 3 feet wide at the midsection.

Baby crocodiles and baby alligators are the exact same
size at the time of hatching—about 9 inches long. They
grow approximately one foot in length each year. Baby
crocodiles are brown with brown blotches. Baby alligators
have distinctive black and yellow stripes on their tails.

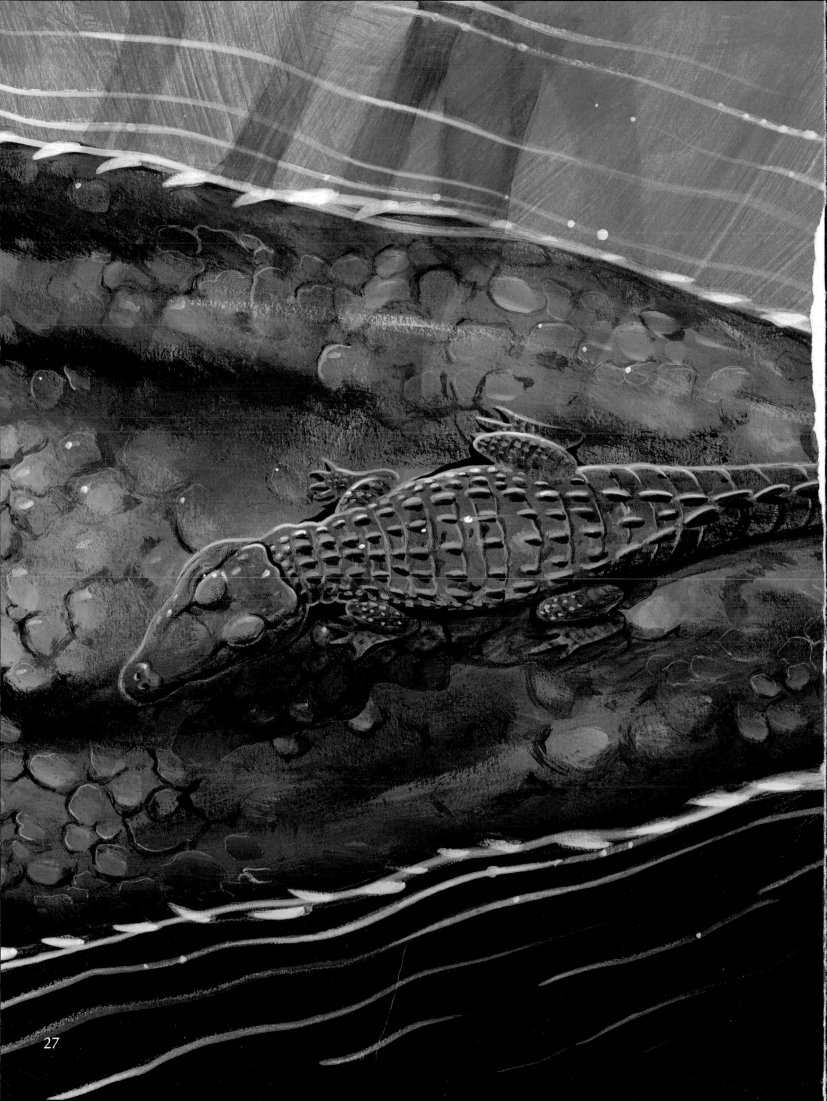

BURMESE PYTHON

A Richness of Reptiles

There are well over 6,000 species of reptiles in the world, living in the oceans and on all continents except Antarctica. The world is rich with reptiles. Their presence fills any outing with a sense of excitement. At any moment, something very much alive and wild may slither or crawl by your feet, sending shivers up your spine.

Recently, while hiking through a tropical hardwood forest in Key Largo, Florida, I felt that excitement in a big way. I was looking for snakes—in particular, one of the pythons reported to be living there. Pythons are large constrictors closely related to boas. Although they are not native to the United States, pythons descended from illegally released pets have been breeding and thriving in the Florida Everglades for years. Now they have spread southward, invading the tropical hardwoods of Key Largo.

The thought of pythons, some reported to be over 10 feet long, slowed my movement through the forest. It had me looking up at the overhanging branches, as well as down at the coral boulders strewn along the path. I walked watchfully, spotting many small lizards that scurried away before my footsteps. But I saw no snakes that day.

There are many ecological reasons why a python should not be where I was hoping to see one. My conscience told me this. But the adventure lover in me thrilled to the possibility of yet another fascinating reptile in our midst.

AUTHOR'S NOTE

THE QUESTION I AM ASKED most often is, "Are you afraid of snakes?" The answer is yes. I'm a little afraid of all reptiles, but not so afraid that I cannot appreciate their beauty and enjoy watching them.

All reptiles will bite if cornered or threatened. To defend themselves, snakes can do little more than bite. Lizards and turtles not only bite—they can scratch with their sharp toenails. And any bite or scratch from a wild animal can be serious. I do carry a snake-bite kit and know how to use it. But in the event of a bite from a venomous snake, my plan is to get to a hospital as quickly as possible. I try not to get close enough to be bitten. All of my up-close reptile watching is done with binoculars or telephoto camera lenses.

The majority of reptiles in this book were painted from photos or video footage I've taken in wild places all across the country. A number of the rare or exotic reptiles were photographed in zoos or private collections.

My wife, Deanna, and I have searched for reptiles from New England to the Sonoran Desert to the Grand Canyon. We have found them across the Great Plains, the middle South, and in the deep South. Our favorite places to photograph reptiles are in the bayous of Louisiana, Georgia's Okeefenokee Swamp, South Carolina's Four Holes Swamp, and the Florida Everglades. I encourage you to include these amazing locations on your lifetime lists of places to see for yourself.

MORE REPTILE READING

Adler, Kraig, and Halliday, Tim. *Firefly Encyclopedia of Reptiles and Amphibians.*
    Toronto, Ontario: Firefly Books Ltd., 2002.
Arnosky, Jim. *All About Alligators.* New York: Scholastic Nonfiction, 2008.
Arnosky, Jim. *All About Lizards.* New York: Scholastic Nonfiction, 2008.
Arnosky, Jim. *All About Rattlesnakes.* New York: Scholastic Nonfiction, 2008.
Arnosky, Jim. *All About Turtles.* New York: Scholastic Nonfiction, 2008.
Arnosky, Jim. *Babies in the Bayou.* New York: G.P. Putnam's Sons, 2007.
Arnosky, Jim. *Turtle in the Sea.* New York: G.P. Putnam's Sons, 2002.
Halliday, Tim, and O'Shea, Mark. *Smithsonian Handbooks: Reptiles and Amphibians.*
    New York: Dorling Kindersley, Inc., 2001.
McCarthy, Colin. *Eyewitness: Reptile.* New York: Dorling Kindersley Limited, 2000.
National Audubon Society. *Field Guide to Reptiles and Amphibians: North America.*
    New York: Alfred A. Knopf, 2000.
Singer, Marilyn. *Venom.* Plain City, OH: Darby Creek Publishing, 2007.
Wilson, Hannah. *Life-Size Reptiles.* New York: Sterling Publishing Co., Inc., 2007.

METRIC EQUIVALENTS

inches	centimeters	feet	meters	pounds	kilograms
1	2.5	1	0.31	1	45
2	5.1	2	0.61	2	9
3	7.6	3	0.91	10	4.5
4	10.2	4	1.22	100	45
5	12.7	5	1.52	200	91
6	15.2	6	1.83	500	227
7	17.8	7	2.13	1000	450
8	20.3	8	2.44		
9	22.9	9	2.74		
10	25.4	10	3.05